D1824130

THE KINGS OF ISRAEL

a story from The Bible retold by MOLLY COX
illustrated by PAUL BIRKBECK
from the BBC TV series *In the Beginning*

COLLINS ST JAMES'S PLACE LONDON

William Collins Sons & Co Ltd
London · Glasgow · Sydney · Auckland
Toronto · Johannesburg

First published 1978
© Text The British Broadcasting Corporation 1978
© Illustrations Paul Birkbeck 1978

ISBN (hardcover) 0 00 183708 7

Printed in Great Britain by W. S. Cowell Ltd. Ipswich

After Moses died, the Jewish tribes settled down to live in Canaan, the land of their ancestors. They were no longer just a wandering group of herdsmen, but a people living in a country of their own. They called their nation Israel, which means in Hebrew "the strength of God". The history of their nation is written in the Bible. It is a strange collection of stories: side by side with the history of wars and conquests, great kings and powerful princes, there are many stories about the God of Israel and the wise men of God, the prophets.

The Israelites once made solemn promises to God to follow his laws and be his people, but they often forgot this agreement. The prophets came to them like messengers from God, to remind them of it, and show them the way back to the Lord God they had promised to trust.

This is the story of some of the kings and prophets of Israel.

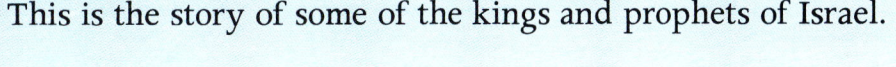

As time went by the Israelites decided, like the other nations around them, to have a king to rule over them; so they asked the holy prophet Samuel to choose who should be their king and to dedicate him to the honour of God. Samuel chose Saul to be king and solemnly anointed him with precious oils, as a sign of God's favour. And all the people shouted, "Long live the King!", because Saul was a fine-looking man, head and shoulders taller than anyone else in the land. But years later when the prophet Samuel was an old man the Lord's voice came to him saying "Saul, the King you anointed, has turned against me: he has rejected me and no longer follows my ways. I have already chosen the future King for my people. Now you, Samuel, must go to a place called Bethlehem, and there I will show him to you."

So Samuel went to Bethlehem and saw a boy called David, looking after his father's sheep, and at once he recognized that this boy was the chosen one of God. So he anointed David with holy oil, and from that day on the power of the Lord was with David. And Samuel went back to his own home, his work completed.

But away in his palace, King Saul sat alone, tormented by such dark thoughts that nothing but music would ease his troubled mind. So they sent for David, the shepherd boy from Bethlehem, to come and play sweet music for the King, and soon Saul grew calm again. And he demanded that David should remain in the palace always to be near him.

At that time, Israel was at war with the Philistines and the day came when the two armies faced each other to do battle. Then one man stepped out from the ranks of the Philistines. He was their champion, a giant of a man called Goliath. He shouted at the Israelites, taunting them:

"Slaves!" he called out, "Is there a man among you who will dare fight me?"

But not one of the Israelites was brave enough to take up the challenge, except David, who set out alone. He wore no armour, and carried neither sword nor shield. But in his hand he held his shepherd's staff, and at his belt was a sling and a bag with five white stones in it.

Goliath was angry when he saw David and shouted, "Do you think I am a dog, that you can come out here and beat me with your stick?" And he cursed him and his people. But David said, "I may not have a sword, but I have come here to kill you, so that all the world will know the power of the God of Israel."

And he put one of the stones in his sling and shot it at the giant, who fell to the ground dead, hit on the forehead by the stone. At once the whole Philistine army turned and fled.

David returned to the palace, no longer a boy, but a
warrior and a hero. And Saul's son, Jonathan, gave
him his own sword and shield to wear, because he
loved him like a brother. But when the King saw how
much all the people loved David and sang his praises
and called him their champion, he was in a rage of
jealousy, and he took up his spear and threw it at him,
to try to kill him.

That night, David fled from the palace, and in the
darkness of the woods Jonathan was waiting for him.

"You must go and hide away in some secret place,"
said Jonathan. "My father is determined to kill you,
because now he knows that you will be the next
king in Israel."

Before they parted, they took an oath to remain
true to each other always, and then David went away
into the hills to escape from Saul. But soon he heard
that the King and his men were out hunting for him,
to kill him, so he went to hide among the rocks
in a cave.

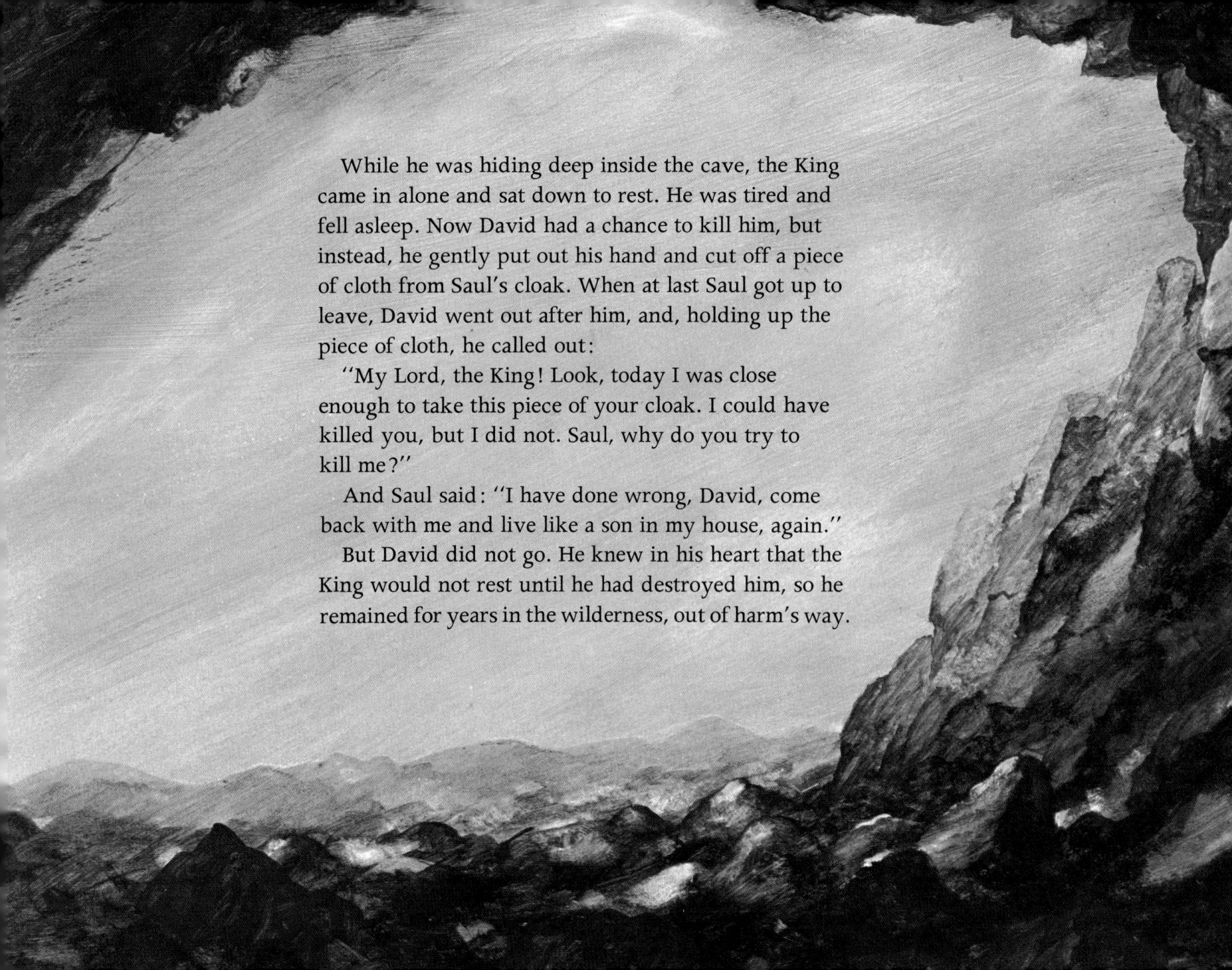

While he was hiding deep inside the cave, the King came in alone and sat down to rest. He was tired and fell asleep. Now David had a chance to kill him, but instead, he gently put out his hand and cut off a piece of cloth from Saul's cloak. When at last Saul got up to leave, David went out after him, and, holding up the piece of cloth, he called out:

"My Lord, the King! Look, today I was close enough to take this piece of your cloak. I could have killed you, but I did not. Saul, why do you try to kill me?"

And Saul said: "I have done wrong, David, come back with me and live like a son in my house, again."

But David did not go. He knew in his heart that the King would not rest until he had destroyed him, so he remained for years in the wilderness, out of harm's way.

Then one day a soldier from Saul's army came to look for David. He told him that a terrible battle had taken place: the Israelites had been defeated and Saul and Jonathan and all his family were dead. And David wept and said:

"Daughters of Israel, weep for Saul,
Who clothed you in scarlet and gold,
And Jonathan who lies dead in a high place.
I am desolate for you, Jonathan, my brother,
Very dear have you been.
Your love to me more wonderful
Than the love of a woman.
Now, the heroes are all fallen
And their weapons have failed."

And the soldier presented David with the royal crown that had fallen from Saul's head, and he was declared King of Israel. He chose Jerusalem for his own city, and he gave orders that the golden shrine Moses had once made should be brought there. In the shrine were kept the written laws of God. And there in Jerusalem before their shrine, the people danced and sang to a great din of trumpets.

And the Lord God blessed King David, and, as was the custom with the kings of those days, he had many wives and many sons and daughters.

One year, when the spring came, the Israelite army went away to do battle, but this time David stayed behind in Jerusalem.

One evening, as he was walking in his palace gardens, he caught sight of a woman in a nearby house. She was bathing in a pool and David saw that she was very beautiful, and he wanted her for himself. Her name was Bathsheba and she was the wife of one of the men who was away fighting with the army. So, in secret, David gave orders that her husband was to be sent to the very front of the battle where he would face the fiercest fighting and risk death. When he heard that his plot had succeeded and the soldier was dead, David took Bathsheba and made her his own wife.

The prophet Nathan heard of what David had done and came to him and said: "In a certain city there were two men, one was rich and the other poor. The rich man had flocks of sheep and herds of cattle, but the poor man had only one little ewe-lamb, which he cared for like a child. One day the rich man was preparing a feast for his friends and did not want to take one of his own animals, so he stole the poor man's only lamb and killed it for his feast."

David was angry. "Show me this man," he said. "By the living God, he deserves to die!"

"You are that man," said Nathan. "You stole that soldier's wife and secretly had him killed; you, whom God himself chose to be King of Israel, have done this thing which he hates. You acted in secret, but he will act in the broad light of the sun; from henceforth the sword will never leave your household."

And David was ashamed, and night and day he prayed:

"Have mercy on me, O Lord!
In your goodness forgive me,
And blot out my guilt.
Help me to learn the secrets of your wisdom,
And renew in me a faithful heart.
So that I can teach wrong-doers your ways,
And show sinners they may turn to you again."

When David was an old man, he sent for his young son Solomon, and said to him: "In my life, I have waged many wars and shed much blood. I am not worthy to build a house for the shrine of the Lord God. But you, my son, when you are King, you must be a man of peace and build an exceedingly magnificent house for the Lord."

So when Solomon became King, he began to build a temple in Jerusalem. Inside, among the rich hangings, the giant candles, the pillars of bronze and the great golden lamps, was the shrine that Moses had made. Inside that shrine lay nothing but the simple slabs of stone on which were written God's rules for a good life.

When the great building was complete, the priests of the temple sounded their trumpets and all the people of Jerusalem came there to sing the Lord's praises. And in front of them King Solomon lifted up his arms and prayed: "O Lord God of Israel, you are so mighty that even heaven and the highest heaven are not vast enough to contain you. I would be foolish, indeed, to think that this house that I have built could be large enough to hold you; but Lord, when your people come to this place to pray, hear them and forgive them."

From then on kings from all over the world came to visit
Solomon, the great King of Israel. They came to see the
wonders of his city, and his palaces were filled with their
presents: gold and silver, ivory and apes and peacocks. Year
by year, he grew richer and his city grew more splendid.

But as he got older, King Solomon the magnificent also turned away from the God of his fathers, and in his heart he began to follow the gold and silver gods of Babylon. Indeed, for all the people, wealth, luxury and power became more important than the promises they had once made to the Lord their God.

When Solomon died, the kings that came after him sold some of the treasures of the temple to pay their soldiers to go to war. The people, too, turned away from God: they preferred a life of wealth and power. The laws of Moses were forgotten. The poor were neglected and made into slaves. Statues of idols were put up in the courtyard of the temple, and people practised witchcraft and the evil arts. Sometimes they even sacrificed their own sons and daughters to try to please the false idols.

But always, in every generation, some people – the wise prophets – remained true to the Lord. Over and over again, they would come like messengers from God to warn the people of Jerusalem to remember the promises their ancestors had made, and listen to the words of God. But the people closed their ears to them.

Then, at last, the prophet Jeremiah stood up inside the gates of the temple and called out in a loud voice: "People of Jerusalem! This is what God says: Sons of Israel, you have broken your agreement with me. You have forgotten my words. You have stolen from the poor, you have shed the blood of children. Now, the army of the King of Babylon will come down on this land with famine and the sword, and its people will be carried off into slavery and Jerusalem will be destroyed. It is the Lord who speaks."

The people crowded round him. They were angry and wanted to drag him down. But Jeremiah said, "Kill me if you dare, but remember, the things I say to you are the things God sent me to say."

Then, what Jeremiah prophesied happened. The armies of the King of Babylon entered Jerusalem. They tore down the temple of Solomon and set fire to the city and killed all whom they found, until in the city there was nothing left.

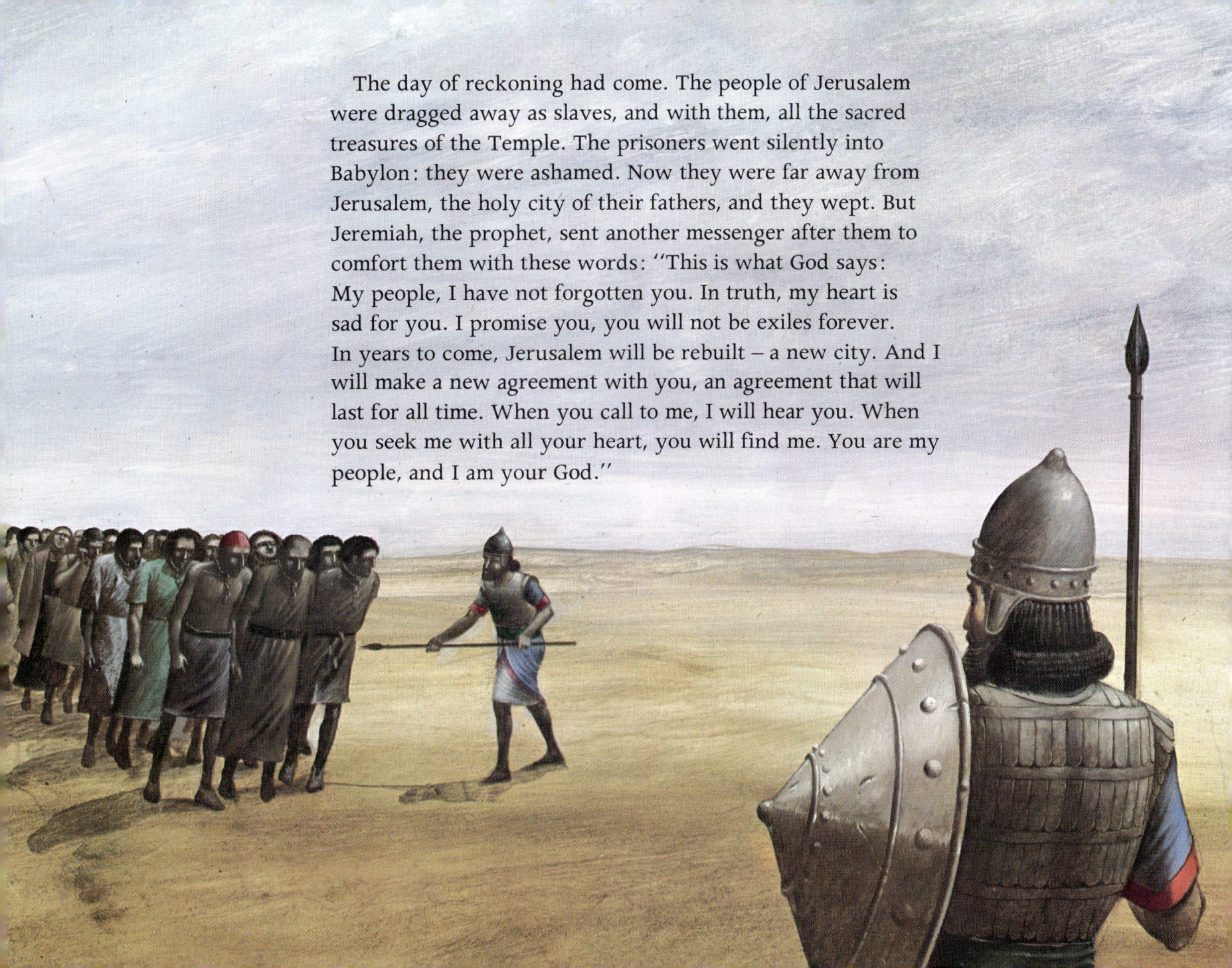

The day of reckoning had come. The people of Jerusalem were dragged away as slaves, and with them, all the sacred treasures of the Temple. The prisoners went silently into Babylon: they were ashamed. Now they were far away from Jerusalem, the holy city of their fathers, and they wept. But Jeremiah, the prophet, sent another messenger after them to comfort them with these words: "This is what God says: My people, I have not forgotten you. In truth, my heart is sad for you. I promise you, you will not be exiles forever. In years to come, Jerusalem will be rebuilt – a new city. And I will make a new agreement with you, an agreement that will last for all time. When you call to me, I will hear you. When you seek me with all your heart, you will find me. You are my people, and I am your God."

Blessed be the Lord, God of Israel,
Let the whole world be filled with his glory.

In the mountains, people will find his peace
And in the little hills, his justice.
For his justice lasts from generation to generation,
His peace remains as long as the sun gives its light.

Every nation in the world shall praise him,
Kings will fall down to do him homage,
He will hold dominion from sea to sea,
From the banks of the great river to the edge of the world.

Yet he hears the helpless when they cry out,
And takes pity on the oppressed.
He sets the poor free from the shackles of violence
And takes their lives into his own care.

His name will be blessed for ever,
His name will endure until the moon is no more.